THE EMOTIONS OF LOVE

Edited by

Heather Killingray

First published in Great Britain in 2004 by
ANCHOR BOOKS
Remus House,
Coltsfoot Drive,
Peterborough, PE2 9JX
Telephone (01733) 898102

All Rights Reserved

Copyright Contributors 2004

SB ISBN 1 84418 378 5

FOREWORD

Anchor Books is a small press, established in 1992, with the aim of promoting readable poetry to as wide an audience as possible.

We hope to establish an outlet for writers of poetry who may have struggled to see their work in print.

The poems presented here have been selected from many entries, and as always editing proved to be a difficult task.

I trust this selection will delight and please the authors and all those who enjoy reading poetry.

Heather Killingray
Editor

Contents

Title	Author	Page
Someone To Hold	Sharon Atkinson	1
When I Close My Eyes	Lisa S Marzi	2
Moonlight	Rosemary Davies	3
Unrequited Love	Simon P Jones	4
The Small House Next-Door To Your Heart	Mary Buckley-Clarke	6
My Love	Robin Morgan	7
Barrier	Rebecca Connery	8
Take Care	Carla Iacovetti	9
Living In Hope . . .	Rosie Hues	10
As I Journey On	Kenneth Mood	11
Scorches Of Love	Anyatonwu Ikechukwa Collins	12
Saturday Love	A Creighton	13
Heaven-Sent	Alana More	14
You, I And We	L J Cowl	15
The Little Steps	John Barnetson	16
The Forgotten Land	Christina Earl	17
Never Surrender	Don Remlart	18
Inspired By An Angel	Andrew Christie	20
My Dearest Darling	Sarah Beck	21
As Love Lay Bleeding	Julie Walker-Daniel	22
A Lover's Lament	Marjorie J Picton	23
The Travelling Thoughts	Juliet Tune	24
My Angel	Jean Bailey	25
To Marjorie	G R Bell	26
My Love, My Life	Charles Peachey	27
Twenty/Twenty	Tom Bissell	28
Fragile Diamonds	Helen Marshall	29
X	Anne-Marie Lloyd-Barrett	30
Lost In Admiration	Geoff Carnall	31
Latin Rhythm	Jacqui Beddow	32
Passing	Alistair McLean	33
My Love	Maggie Strong	34
The Spitfire Pilot	Maureen Reynolds	35
Come And Go	Alan Zoltie	36

Title	Author	Page
Deep Love	Stephen C Matthews	37
A Love Lost, A Love Found	Andrew John Stevenson	38
Only Words	Paul Burton	39
For Mary	Roland Richmond	40
Passion	Michael Close	41
Are You Mine	R Nelson	42
Tell Me	Karen Williams	43
Obsession	Mary Smythe	44
First Love	Alexa Crawford	45
The Vision	K Copley	46
Chain Reaction Of Love	David Charles	47
Of Love Damned	L Joseph	48
Trust	Lee Byway	49
Love	Helena A P Goncalves	50
Love's Dream	Nigel Basher	51
Secret Dreams	Margaret Parnell	52
Rebecca	Simon Raymond McCreedy	53
Love Letter	Madeline Morris	54
A Haiku Promise - Lo, I Am With You Always	G A Baker	55
Repeated Repetition	Frank Littlewood	56
Distances	Eve M Turner	57
I Could Only Stand And Stare	Mary Baird Hammond	58
Echoes	Richard Gould	59
Too Little Too Late	Jill Lowe	60
I've Loved A Few Times	M Woolvin	61
Beauty - I've See The Rarest Beauty Of All	Keith Jackson	62
Die For Love	Natalie Biagioni	63
Blind Date	A Hyde Murphy	64
Take Note	Sue Woodbine	65
She Pines	J E Kirkman	66
Sorrow Hollow	Alan Pow	67
Fragile	John Bilven Morin	68
Empty The Day	Nigel Davies	69
Heartbreak's Light	Marty Grief	70
Space	Carol Spencer	71
A Summer Rhapsody	S H Smith	72

End Of The Game	Ann Blair	73
The Lowest Time Of My Life	Louise Allen	74
Recital	Christopher W Wolfe	75
How Can I?	Danielle Watts	76
I'm Under Your Spell	Patricia Green	77
Elegy To Love	Fraser Hicks	78
Eternal Desire	Peter Steele	79
Without You	Julia Smith	80
When Two Become One	April Dickinson-Owen	82
A Love Affair	Marjorie Busby	83
Heartsease	Geraint Jenkins	84
Temptation Of An Orange	Juliet Marshall	85
Autobiography	Bill Austin	86
The Magnet	Clive Goldsmith	87
Animal Instinct	Theresa Griffiths	88
Suzanne	Kevon Hayhoe	89

SOMEONE TO HOLD

I don't ask for much
Just happiness and friendship
Is it too much to ask
When I am feeling low
That someone just cradle me in their arms
And holds me
Hugs me
Fills me with warmth
And stop the tears from falling
They say there is someone for everybody
I don't think I want love
Love normally leads to hurt and pain
I just want to be held
Will someone hold me please?

Sharon Atkinson

WHEN I CLOSE MY EYES

'When I close my eyes,
I see your eyes,
as dark pools of love,
penetrating my being -
I see your warm smile,
radiating like the sun,
beckoning me to you,
to experience those tender
moments of love,
when I can feel your breath on my cheek,
leading to those nights of passion,
everlasting in my memory,
this is ecstasy at its best,
and loneliness at its worst!'

'Now I am back in your arms again,
feeling your caresses embracing me all over,
if only for a short time,
like a 'serene overcoat',
harbouring me from the 'storms of life',
as 'our world' transcends time,
where past and present intermingle,
and true love knows no boundaries -
tears having been shed for eternity,
with the scent of your touch lingering on.'

'Suddenly I open my eyes,
And your face is gone,
But only momentarily,
As it is forever etched into my soul,
Until the next time -
When I close my eyes!'

Lisa S Marzi

MOONLIGHT

In the darkness I undress for bed,
On the pillow I lay down my head.
Just as I'm drifting off to sleep,
The moon decides to take a peep.

At midnight her face shines so bright,
The room is bathed in her frosty light.
As I watch with quiet fascination,
She is dancing in my imagination.

Her shimmering icy beams,
Hold me spellbound lost in dreams.
A magical moment suspended in time,
Transported into enchantment sublime.

Suddenly the room is black as night,
The moon is hidden from my sight.
Playing hide and seek with the clouds,
When she reappeared I laughed out loud.

After I'd watched her for an age,
I realise that the sky is her stage.
Her last performance is an encore,
She disappears to be seen no more.

Rosemary Davies

UNREQUITED LOVE

When I first knew you, the floodgates opened,
Then you went and broke my heart,
You said you would stay, through sunshine, rain and snow,
Then you played with my mind,
Forever is such a little word,
But it's so powerful it hurts,
The canyon of my golden heart is deep but meaningless,
And the corrie within my guilt-edge emotion,
Often overflows into saltlets of shame-ridden tears,
I know I am so lucky to be alive,
But memories of your loving arms that once embraced me,
Return to fill my soul with a kind of pain,
That I once thought I had kissed goodbye forever.

Life is short, eternity is long,
So maybe I can take comfort in that,
But every time I see the morning star,
Shining graceful and serene,
Every time I smile through my fears,
Every time I am terrified of myself,
Every time I take my pills and potions,
I could go on forever,
But one day soon, a change is going to come,
One day, maybe the best writer ever known,
Will appear, like a light in the storm,
Like a hand held out to those afraid of drowning,
Like a meal for the millions who are starving,
Maybe, it's true, after all -
That He loves us, wants us and maybe even needs us.

But the golden embers in my heart remain,
A reflection of a face that I see dimly and dark,
I look in the mirror but I don't recognise myself,
I look in your sky, but it's forever raining,
I sense a need to have compassion on my own emotions,
After all, I am a child of the universe,
And I belong to this wild and wonderful world,

After all I'm not the only one with a broken soul.

So I will lift my spirit - no matter how torrential,
The winter storms maybe,
Until spring appears with its buds and blooms,
Until spring melts into summer,
Until summer fades into autumn.

Then perhaps I will be able to express,
All those things that kept me chained to feeling free,
And free to feeling chained.

Then perhaps my self-pity will lose pride of place,
And maybe my self-esteem will grow,
Until I remember you without crying.

This bruised soul bears scars like -
A butcher's board bear cuts,
But it's all ifs, buts and maybes, Dear God, can you see?

Simon P Jones

THE SMALL HOUSE NEXT-DOOR TO YOUR HEART

The roses have folded their petals,
The ladybird hides 'neath the leaf,
And all of the fairies are grouping
On the lawn of our home as we sleep.
There's a house with a door that is golden,
Inside a white unicorn lives,
She sleeps on a deep bed of daisies
That has smocking of daffodil frills.

And no one can go there but you, love,
For nobody else has the chart.
And a little shy unicorn lives there
In the small house, next-door to your heart.
Push the door gently, it's open,
The unicorn waits just inside,
Whisper your wishes, she's waiting it seems
To carry you off on a ride.

Away to the land of the dreamer,
With stars falling 'way from her hooves
To fields of warm snow, where marshmallows grow,
She will take you wherever you choose.
You can rest when adventures are over,
Lie by her side for awhile.
I will see you are hearing her heartbeat
In the soft, gentle kiss of your smile.

And no one can go there but you love,
For nobody else has the chart.
And nobody else holds the key, love,
To the dreams that you own from the start.
I will lift you and hold you my darling,
Glad as another day starts,
But, know that the unicorn's waiting
In the small house next-door to your heart.

Mary Buckley-Clarke

MY LOVE

You are like a rose of shimmering beauty
fresh as the morning dew,
a rose so soft and tender,
with a heart so pure and true,
a rose that always blossoms,
a rose that never dies,
for deep down inside of me,
next to my heart it lies.

Robin Morgan

BARRIER

There is a wall between us.
Glass.
I can see you and you watch me,
But we do not touch.
We cannot touch.
It is forbidden by those who do not wish it.
Including your observer.
And mine.

I could leave if I want to.
If I wanted to.
You would just watch me,
Your speech impaired,
Craving to say what we will not speak.
But I am caught here.
And so are you. Eternally.

We have been this way
For as long as I can remember
And I do not want it to end.
It is what I live for.
To tease you
And to be teased.

Rebecca Connery

TAKE CARE

Take care, do not lose your heart
in the mad dash to be someone,
for life has a way of diminishing
the voice of longing, eroding
and replacing the inner soul
with driven ness, busyness
and a million dos and don'ts,
while we grow to be deaf, suppressing
longing, living in the external
pretentious place as we are masked
with a facade that all is well.
Take care, not to annul your heart
where substance and reality stem
out of the inner place of sanctity;
burying things important, creating
duplicity and our sense of passion,
dreams, adventure and mystery
are squelched between agendas,
stubborn pride, programs, methodology
and desire becomes a flavour you choose
for ice cream and longing can be
managed, given the right strategy.
Take care, not to lose sight of
things important, things lasting,
even eternal in the attempt to
keep everything under control;
forgetting desire, poetry, art,
melodies that fill a soul, intrigue,
ecstasy, passion and the ability
to truly be intimate in friendship
or in love, drifting far away
from the heart's shore, missing out
on true happiness, trading our
souls for compromise.

Carla Iacovetti

LIVING IN HOPE...

The pen lay down with the softest of sighs,
Laid down by the broken heart.
Neither had strength to communicate
For both had been torn apart.
The heart, so broken, had looked to the pen,
A glimmer of hope there remained.
If only the pen would talk for the heart,
If it communicated for the pained.
The heart knows now that the pen did that
Tho t'was twenty odd years ago.
But the pen told people who wouldn't care,
And in those times that the pen did not know.
Now! Like the phoenix up from the ashes,
Up rises the pen with the heart.
They talk and flow of the things they know.
Knowing at last they never can part.
'Tis when the heart is full up to bursting,
The pen rises to take up the strain.
They flow together with feeling,
And as they flow they flow away pain.
The pen has turned into a rainbow,
The heart has turned that way too.
They grow bolder now they have a future.
Full of promises all to come true.
               By The Grace Of God . . .

Rosie Hues

AS I JOURNEY ON

My love is growing stronger
And I love my wife even more.
The joy my children are bringing
Is full of supernatural things.
I appreciate each day
Because it's like a treasure chest full of dreams.

My love is overflowing
And my body, mind and spirit
Shows me more of the truth each week.
I can relax more and enjoy
The book of life, unfolding,
Thank you God for the love you are giving.

Kenneth Mood

SCORCHES OF LOVE

So trusted and held in esteem,
Lives my love and dream,
At a time of scorching season,
She deserted me devoid of reason.
And slays me with pleasing pain,
I laughed and hope of having my gain
But thumps and bumps are in love so trusted
Just like sob smiling in marriage so frustrated.
The unexamined love can bite,
But always in decorated spite,
Watching her victim in sordid state.
O' strong is the scourges of love's pet.

Anyatonwu Ikechukwa Collins

SATURDAY LOVE

Sat in a room,
On a dull Saturday,
Thinking of you,
So far away,
Aching for touches,
The thrill of your lips,
The strain of it all,
Seems far too much,
Stomach is knotted,
Mouth becomes dry,
Feelings for you,
Rush in,like a tide,
Need just to hold you,
Let emotions subside
To leave when they're gone,
Sensations so true,
A feeling of love,
Meant only for you,
But, you are not here,
The dream it must wait,
The day is so long,
And empty, with no you.

A Creighton

HEAVEN-SENT

So lucky am I that you came by,
To spark my soul that longed to die.
An angel's kiss is what you give,
An innocence warming me to live.
The stars are yours so bright, so pure,
I'll love you until they shine no more.
Such radiance has a hold of you,
I never felt such love so true.
I bless the day that you were born,
Darkness for me was truly forlorn.
The skies opened up and the heavens shined,
Or so I felt when I first saw your smile.
So lucky am I that you came by,
My angel, my daughter, some day you will fly.

Alana More

YOU, I AND WE

When I'm broken, it's you who fixes me
And when I'm sleeping, you are there;
Coiled around me,
A cloak from darkness,
A filter for my air.

The roots beneath my apple tree,
You choose the soil and let me bloom.
Gliding in love's fluid
We are the twins inside the womb.

I'm a blank canvas you dressed in colour,
The pacing tiger you freed from the zoo;
The healer who cured the blind man,
And all that I am is you.

L J Cowl

THE LITTLE STEPS

Every day we are together, we take a little step,
closer to each other from the day that we first met.
We started out as just good friends, we planned it from the start,
we left it to the little steps, to guide our loving hearts.

Every day we are together, we take a little step,
as we learn new things about each other, with each other
we are less inept.
Each step together finds common ground, on which
our friendship's based,
important little steps these are, our foundations are better placed.

Every day we are together, we take a little step,
each step becomes more intimate, each step becomes more heartfelt.
Our feelings for each other, now surface to the fore,
from like to love, they're changing form, our love is growing more.

Every day we are together, we take a little step,
our love for each other is quickening pace, from each other
we can't be kept.
Our love is growing ever stronger, to blossom like a flower,
when we're apart, we pine away, whilst counting down the hours.

Every day we are together, we take a little step,
our love for each other is so complete, no hint of doubt now left.
We pledge our love implicitly, as if they were marriage vows,
so let the little steps guide our future, while we live for the here
and now.

John Barnetson

THE FORGOTTEN LAND

Your smile overpowers,
Full of light,
It shimmers,
Contagious to every soul.

The tunnel lightens,
My future there glimmers,
Like a magical illusion,
It sparkles and shines.

A glimpse of glitter,
A glisten and glow,
Something of mine,
To cherish forever.

A light in the darkness,
A helping hand,
A heartbeat that brightens,
The Forgotten land.

Christina Earl

NEVER SURRENDER

Pretty princess of prince 'Pascat',
Your boundless bunch of beauty
Dazzling deep down my heart,
I'm frenzy, crazy in your presence
By your silk skin and curvaceous back.

Fragrances that flow at your arrival
Are so lovely than the one manoeuvre
Never will pettish prompted me to another.
Kindly kindle hope in my tingling heart
Wherever, whenever, I'll be there till ever.

Though there is no specific simile
That can really express my emotion,
Metaphor and alliteration are not suitable
Yet in words will I convey my motion
As to fulfil my main mission;

Sort of song can it win your heart,
Sort of surprise, can it pierces your soul?
Wearing weird on your face
Each time I tend to move closer,
But never will I let my mission pass.

Oh! In your absence I seemed complete
But my life is purely incomplete
Yet I'll never surrender nor relent
For sometime someday will I be victorious
Surely as you remain the only masterpiece.

Ready to do anything you want,
Even if you leave in the den
Willing will I enter a lair
Definitely my survival is not sure
But it's you I love and curiously care.

Upon Cupid and Venus I call
To make dearer to your heart
My lasting love in haste;
To hold and hang me to your heart
For you to be mine and only mine . . .

Don Remlart

INSPIRED BY AN ANGEL
(Dedicated to Melanie May)

There are some words in life,
Words that mean so little and those that can mean so much,
Words that can make us laugh and make us cry,
Words that tell truth and can tell a lie,
Words that describe who we are,
Words that dictate our inner power,
Words that can destroy but can also heal,
Words that rhyme and save us time,
Words that can comfort and guide,
Words can tell us so much,
Words are spoken from the mouth but come from the heart,
These are the words that I have for you . . .
I love you.

Andrew Christie

MY DEAREST DARLING

As I stand in the field of roses,
the sun sets and the darkness encloses,
the moon creeps out and I see you again,
your radiant beauty in the rain.
Every night I see you cry,
you turn your head as though you're shy,
you look at me with your pale blue eyes,
as though to say, 'Please, no lies.'
A tear trickles down my cheek,
the wind blows your hair, so soft and sleek,
I cannot bring myself to say those words,
I hear the tweet of birds.
You sigh and begin to go,
my time is way too low,
'Stop,' I cry, 'listen, this is true,
My dearest darling, I love you.'

Sarah Beck (12)

AS LOVE LAY BLEEDING

This aching heart, forgotten feeling
    Returns once more.
Dark days and silent nights provide no healing
    Yet you had the gore
Pretending as love lay bleeding.
    A disregarded ring
But, still we hold on to a prayer and a wing.

This angel's truth, begotten grief
    Surrenders its soul.
Love and light enters with great eve
    But I become whole.
Searching for the truth, now the world
    And its wife can see
At last, the lies will subside and my heart finally set free.

Julie Walker-Daniel

A Lover's Lament

I composed another little song, in memory of my love,
And sang it in the woodlands, to echo up above.
I shouted out my secret, but no one there could hear,
Would my lover come to me? My eyes did shed a tear.
I sang it to the trees, to the flowers I confessed,
How very much I loved her when our marriage vows were blessed.
I sang it to the sky, but the clouds just veiled her face,
Her beauty hidden by the mist, yet still so full of grace.
I shouted to the sea, where shimmering waves did prance,
And on the surf that lapped the shore, her golden feet would dance.
Yet in this simply pensive mood, I sang and walked alone,
Would I meet my love again? The one I called my own.

The golden sun was setting, and everything was calm,
And softly in the summer air, the gentle breeze was warm.
Perhaps I felt so negative, that I had failed somehow,
I'd strived so much for happiness, and made one single vow.
Then strangeness came, then silence, a bright and shining light,
Would my lover come to me, to share this lonely night?
I felt her love around me, she came to me at last,
And held her tightly in my arms - the lovers' spell was cast.
Then I sang my song to her, and kissed her on her cheek,
United now together, united in one peace.
In my secret mind I wished for most - the answer's simply this
That we remain together still enraptured in true bliss.

Tomorrow - tomorrow - tomorrow
Into
Eternity.

Marjorie J Picton

THE TRAVELLING THOUGHTS

High, high atop the sky
A dense-grey matter lies
Once through this
There is a place
Where my beloved abides.

Unsure how travelling thoughts go by
The massive wedge between the skies
Or how it is that he awoke
And changed the darkness
Into hope.

He's not exactly
Who I knew
But one thing stayed the same
From dust to dust
Love will survive
If we take what still remains.

Juliet Tune

MY ANGEL

Like a rose bud you turned into a beautiful rose, I loved to brush
your hair and when you were sad I wiped away your tears
as they fell like the morning dew.

Your smile is like an angel and you have a heart made of gold,
I look to you like a star in the sky, 'you shine' my darling babe,
my little princess with hair like gold.

Like a child you still stand now with children of your own young
and still so beautiful, everybody's friend. Thank God he answered
my prayers and gave you back to the world for my sake.

Jean Bailey

TO MARJORIE

When hand in hand we walked
Fingers interlocked
we were content.
When arm in arm we strolled
there was no need for words.
When we embraced
your fragrant hair
lay soft against my face
and young love sparkled in our eyes.
But, that was nineteen forty-eight,
and now,
when hand in hand we walk
Fingers interlocked
we are content.
When arm in arm we stroll
there is no need for words.
When we embrace
your silver hair
lies soft against my face
and through our eyes the old love shines.
Young love, old love,
real love will never change.

G R Bell

MY LOVE, MY LIFE

Your silver hair once brown and bright,
Is still more lovely in my sight,
And when you smile, your eyes do shine,
I thank my God that you are mine.

We met when you were just fourteen,
A bonnier girl I had never seen,
Each time I saw you, right from the start,
An extra beat came into my heart.

You are my sunshine, I feel so warm,
You're like my protector, I fear no harm,
You are my night-time, my restful sleep,
We share a love that runs oh so deep.

You are my laughter, I love you to smile,
You make me feel good, just talking awhile,
You are my voice, I want to sing like a lark,
You light up my life, when it all turns dark.

My

  D on't ever doubt that I love you
  O ver anyone else in this world
  R ight from the 'first night' I saw you
  I 've had my poor heart in a whirl
  S houting 'my love's' just for you.

Charles Peachey

TWENTY/TWENTY

I awoke from my sleep and carried on dreaming,
An angel appeared and I gave up my soul.
Your beauty shines through and it gives my life meaning,
You are my parts, my sum and my whole.
Your love has enslaved me, I give you control.

Life contains wonders, amazement and grace,
There are things which will always be true,
Creation, has given, a vision to guide us,
My perfect vision is you.

The feeling I get waking up by your side,
Cannot be spoken or captured and written.
When you are near beauty won't be denied,
A world now a pleasure to live in,
I thank you for all that you don't know you've given.

A summertime spectacle, an open air show,
A sunset's design to tame the sky blue.
Creation, has given, a vision to guide us,
My perfect vision is you.

The sun would still rise, were you to leave,
The world would still turn and life would go on.
A difference this time, because this pain is mine,
Without you, my reason has gone.
Nothing else matters. You are the one.

Without intervention, the stars always shine,
The tides are controlled by the moon.
Creation, has given, a vision to guide us,
My perfect vision is you.

To know of existence, appreciate life,
Is to witness a miracle set to.
Creation, has given, a vision to guide us,
But I don't see a thing, I'm looking at you.

Tom Bissell

FRAGILE DIAMONDS

I didn't realise it was so safe,
Now I see it needed a reason to be,
But now that is all obsolete,
Now only the paper remains,
And the paper remains will become torn,
Torn like the angel in me,
In the ashes of our memories.

Helen Marshall

X

I stand and watch you while you sleep,
Then in your room I gently creep.
Kneeling beside you on the floor,
Want to be near you as before.

But as I awake my dreams collapse,
You want no more, I am your past.
My heart aches, it's cracked in two,
Knowing I've lost you to someone new.

I hope she loves you like I do,
With heart and mind and soul so true.
Then part of me can rest,
I know at least, I've done my best.

Anne-Marie Lloyd-Barrett

LOST IN ADMIRATION

How fiercely
Love's flame
Can burn
Bringing happiness
And sorrow
In their turn.

How quickly
Love can
Inspire
There are no
Boundaries
To desire.

How tempting
Love's passion
Can rage
With desire.

How gently
Through the night
Lovers lips
Unite.

How sadly
Lovers lives
Expire
Love's flame
Still burning
With desire.

Geoff Carnall

LATIN RHYTHM

Latin lover can't you see
The music's in my soul
Come closer, hold me tight and
Feel the rhythm flow.

As the beat gets faster
Our bodies intertwine
All the time the music flows
Like liquid golden wine.

Feel the heat, the mood is right
The pace is getting faster
Latin lover come to me and
Move a little closer

I feel your heart, your warm embrace
As we dance like lovers do
The crowd watch with bated breath
For the climax of the show.

The music reaches fever pitch
The drumming a part of us
Dancing, whirling, spinning round
The finale is faultless.

We take our bows, the applause is loud
They all enjoyed the show
The stage is empty now at last
Let's dance our dance of love.

Jacqui Beddow

PASSING

Just like the moonbeams of the night
The lady's eyes always held your sight,
They sparkled on and on and on,
In daylight flew and now she's gone.

To go with that beguiling glance,
Did she not think once of romance?
What of this valley that opened wide,
And took my sense right o'er the side?

Had she no soul, was I just a mat,
To be cast off, and end all that?
Was love allowed, was it a crime?
Perhaps, perhaps . . . some other time.

Alistair McLean

MY LOVE

My love you lay beside me
Your arms so tight embrace me
I thought our love would end dear
As the feuds have been so great dear
But all those thoughts have gone now
This ending of our last row
I hope there'll be no more love
I could not cope with more love.
Your breathing so deep, so fine
And I know you're still mine
All worries gone away
Our love survives another day.
You showed you really love me
How happy I was to see.
All these years together
We've got through all the storms together
And so I lay so tightly embraced
I close my eyes to savour not to waste
This precious moment dear
And whisper I love you dear
To close my eyes and remain
In your arms and not refrain
To stay with you until morn
My love not ended but reborn.

Maggie Strong

THE SPITFIRE PILOT

Alone with his dreams,
The old man
sits in the cafe.
Surrounded by
the bacon rolls
and steamed up windows.

He remembers the plane
and the smell of hot fuel
as he soared through clouds
and scoured the sky.
Below, wide-eyed children gazed in awe
at heroes who saved them from death and the enemy.

Now, the street children
call him names.
A swaggering gang call him
a stupid old fool.
They throw stones through his window
and bricks at his door.

So he sits in the cafe
with tears in his eyes,
amid the foil wrapped butter
and plastic pot jam.
An old hero
alone with his dreams.

Maureen Reynolds

COME AND GO

Tensions at a peak, an end in sight
Built up by touch and verbiage
Situation not ideal for procurement
Lingering doubts spread by continual noise

Windows lowered for ventilation
Upright posture non-conducive to completion
Stimulation encouraged and given
Law enforcement passing regularly

Time ran out, hours passing in seconds
Moving quietly across unexplored terrain
Aroused, with no outlet to vent frustrations
Decisions made to finalise the evening

Darkness found for absolute safety
Happiness arriving fast with delightful satisfaction
Clock now ticking in rhythm with movement
It was time to come and then go.

Alan Zoltie

DEEP LOVE

Forget all the passion, anxiety and pain
Try to respond with strong-minded restrain
For many a person have started to see
That love is not all it is cracked up to be

We all expect too much from the person we seek
Love makes us tired, anxious and weak
Let's try and see what else we could do
To stop the love in our hearts from making us blue

We need and we need but whatever for
It isn't our own love we have to explore
Exactly what is it we have in our mind?
When we realise that knowledge our love we will find

Our hearts are so full and minds so unclear
Why does this deep love have me like this here?
I will never wonder how much you really care
This love's ours my darling, for us both to share.

Stephen C Matthews

A LOVE LOST, A LOVE FOUND

Where did it go? Where has it gone? My love
So strong, it wore my smile, to my partner's delight.
Has it taken wings to fly like the dove?
Did demons take it through the Devil's night?

I awoke close to her, feelings all cold;
She lay there, beautiful, unknowing in sleep!
I buttoned my lips and bade her not to be told,
For my empty heart's secret for now I will keep.

Her eyelids fluttered, she looked while she rose.
Such radiance; could she see? Would she tell!
Bidding her morning my insides froze
For now, how my love lost, I must dwell.

I searched my mind then probed my heart,
Perhaps from a nightmare it was hiding in fright.
Not knowing I had woken, still cowering in the dark,
So wonderful is she; come back I say (my love), heed my plight.

Downcast in sorrow, hands clasped to the sky,
I fell from my steady perch to kneel.
Looking to the heavens I asked my God why
A man in love, was made this to feel.

So caring, giving me a hug for my gloom,
Pulling my weight to her, she held me tight.
In her kiss, my love lost came to bloom;
It was still loving in her from last night.

Andrew John Stevenson

ONLY WORDS

Words were all I had
before you drifted into view.
Words are all I'll ever have
now there's no more 'I love you'.

Letters layered with meaning
infuse my mind with images of us,
twilight together-time
now tainted by disgust.

Words were what you wanted
as it slowly fell apart
but tough talking took us nowhere,
sent us both back to the start.

So I sit here idly scribbling,
thinking only about you
through days devoid of meaning
knowing our love once proved true.

Paul Burton

FOR MARY

How long? How many lifetimes long ago?
    Did your free choice decree my ring's return?
    The torch that burned for you still burns; will burn
'til life's last secret is for me to know.
You gained that knowledge sad long years ago
    and so it is from others I must learn
    what has become of paramount concern -
was your life with him happy - yes or no?
    Your fortune as his wife I nothing knew
        but learned how fierce his hate of me could be
    and guessed with whose kind help that hatred grew
        to crown her spite in taking you from me.
            Once briefly, mine, to you beyond the grave
            always my love; my thanks for all you gave.

Roland Richmond

PASSION

Was I your Romeo, and you my Juliet,
no couple more in love, upon the day we met,
intense the passion burned, within the love we had,
some times so full of tenderness,
some times with rage so bad.

A love match made in Heaven,
a love match made in Hell,
was this the love we wanted,
a thing on which to dwell,
destructive in its own device,
was never open to advice.

Were you and I in love too much,
was passion all but spent,
tempestuous in beginning,
was never heaven sent.

Michael Close

ARE YOU MINE

If only you would say you love me,
If only you would say you care.
Then my heart would know that you love me so,
If only you would say you care.

I swear by all the stars above dear,
That my love for you is true.
And I hope and pray that someday you will say,
That you really love me too.

For I am living for you only,
Without you there's nothing left for me.
It would break my heart if ever we should part,
So darling please say you are mine.

R Nelson

TELL ME

Do you kiss her and
smile your beautiful smile?
Do you stroke her
and tell her she has the softest skin?
Do you wrap your arms around her
and take away her pain?
Do you make love to her
and give her visions of wolves?

Do you miss me?

Karen Williams

OBSESSION

The broken promise of spring
is very human.
Daffodils toss in an unkind wind.

When you are promised the world
you have to accept
mist and malevolence,
cold that bites, the barren margins
and a hopeless dawn
along with the sunlit landscape.

You offer me the world:
you offer me your life.
Included in the package
sulk, storm, torpidity
and the heat
of a hundred volcanoes.

I will take the world
and roll it around my life;
take my life and roll it with yours
snowballing the past,
cut grass and moonlight, music
and all those fingerprints.

The irises you gave as a peace offering
shrivel into fists, a bunch
of defensive knuckles.
I will collect the broken promises
in a matchbox until
they spill
over and require a packing case.
I will nail down the lid
and label it 'Pandora - not to be opened!'

Mary Smythe

FIRST LOVE

Scarlet light fleeting through an invisible sky.
Untraceable ink, linking them together
Today, tomorrow, beyond the reality that you paint and flee,
An emptiness reaches out to me.

An endless possibility of grace and choice,
Voicing both everything and nothing.
All at once you disappear, beneath the image, the illusory life
I created you out of.

Retracting the invitation I lend to you,
The pleas resound throughout the abyss,
Appearing to fade in a single kiss.

Hit or miss that is always the way,
Preserving yourself for another day.

Now I've seen through you,
Gathered my erroneous judgements,
And placed them in front of me.
I have it mapped out - an undefeatable plan to conquer your memory.
You will not bring me back down.
This is my stand.

Alexa Crawford

THE VISION

Those lovely hazel eyes sparkling so bright,
A smile could thrill me anytime.
A voice so mellow like a breath of air,
It could take away all my care.
Your hands so pleasant and smooth to touch,
A welcome that was nice to hear.

As you led into the lounge that day,
'Twas a delight to watch you walk.
The sensuous way you moved along,
Like a swan gliding o'er the pool.
You turned and smiled as I walked through,
As I introduced myself and why I came.

We talked of ways I could help you and Mother,
For her to get a better life somewhere.
All the while you sat in front of me,
With a posture that showed your beauty.
A woman that any man could love,
A slave that would serve you blindly.

Anything I asked of you was dealt with so kindly,
You gave me all I was looking for.
Now as I sit and think of you,
As Christmastime gets nearer.
As I busy myself getting a meal for myself,
I sit and eat it on my own, I won't forget you.

I will drink a toast to those eyes so bright,
As they smiled at me before you.
And when you had a drink of wine,
So gracefully like nectar.
Each move you made, each word you said,
Will remain with me in my heart forever.

K Copley

CHAIN REACTION OF LOVE

Shakespeare's romantic tragedy
'Romeo and Juliet' set five centuries ago
How different is it today - from then
None to be really honest
Do-gooders - parents - want to fix
The lives of the young, with good intention
Juliet's parents tried to fix it for her to marry
Count Paris - a party was set to heal a family feud
But it doesn't go to plan - Romeo went to see his
Love Rosaline - but saw Juliet first
And the rest they say is history - an
Unknown phenomenon - Kismet - no one knows
They married in secret in Verona, we have Gretna
Chinese whispers, cause havoc, messages get lost
No one should go to the extreme, they did, some do
But whether it be rhyme or reason, or religion
Or whether others agree or disagree
Once the seeds of love are sewn, they should
Be left to ripen, whatever the outcome
Gable once said, 'Frankly I don't give a damn'
And to be honest, when love is all around
Quite frankly, I think we all agree

David Charles

OF LOVE DAMNED

Your betrayal is as sharp as an adder
pressing his fangs against my womb

You flay me with your love
'til I am naked and without skin

My eyes were blinded by wings of raven black,
seduced by emerald seas girded by sparkling sands

You paved my road with roses and sweet oils
and led me thus to the slaughter house

Pulsing and throbbing as does the desperate prey
I am running out before a pack of baying hounds

I lay me down in innocence like a lamb
and woke up in the bleakness of desperation

Misery welcomed me with open arms
now when the night dawns, I arise
to partake of your rotting shadow

L Joseph

TRUST

Find it hard to place your trust,
Rock solid faith soon turns to dust.
Unconnected you feel lonesome.

Wish to be in someone's arms,
But you don't want the pain or harm,
Of letting your trust get broken.

Tears drop down and stain your cheek,
Hidden feelings you just won't speak.
Emotionally drained, you feel so weak.

I love you more than life itself,
But blind to my feelings you still can't see.
If you can't trust anyone,
Try trusting me.

Lee Byway

LOVE

When I lay upon my bed
And think of your sweet face,
A more darling man I could not wish
to meet in our human race.

The chemistry between us
is electric, quite exuberant.
At times we've been rumbustious,
Licentious and ebullient!

Phew . . . ?

And when you look upon me,
I tingle, my heart skips,
It feels too good, it cannot be,
Then your lips touch my lips?

I realise, of all the men there are
upon this Earth of ours,
You're the one, I love by far,
You're the man who lights my stars!

Helena A P Goncalves

LOVE'S DREAM

Now that I have found you
I need look no more
For to me you are everything
And all that I have longed for

Love has found me
Or so it would seem
Yet I lie sleeping
And you dwell only in my dreams

Nigel Basher

SECRET DREAMS

The days of wine and roses
Can't last forever,
But memories
Go on to the end of time.
Bittersweet memories
Mingled with lost loves,
We lived for the moments,
Days didn't count.
Moonlight and roses
As we danced away the nights,
Secret havens to hide away
The promises we made.
But like rose petals
Drifted away on a
Warm summer evening breeze.
What happened
To those hazy, crazy summer nights?
Time I'm afraid
Doesn't stand still.
The sands of time
Put an end
To all 'Eastern promises'
As we turn the 'pages of time'.
Memories on every 'line'.

Margaret Parnell

REBECCA

With creation green eyes,
And a smile to melt your heart,
Her amazing, bright spirit,
Is my light when it is dark,
She has taken me from the depths of wrong,
And brought me to the sun,
How empty my life would be,
Without her wonderful love.

Simon Raymond McCreedy

LOVE LETTER

Dear Lover, I write you this letter,
To clear all my thoughts and make me feel better.
See it's you who brought me down to my knees,
A girl who's so wayward and so hard to please.
It's true, I never knew, there could be so much love,
When I am with you.
And I need you, I could never deceive you.
You say you love me and yes, I believe you.
I want you so much, you could not understand,
How I jump at your command, meet your every demand.
My darling, you are my soulmate and friend,
You made a promise, it can't be the end.
But it is, only you could inflict so much pain,
My heart is so heavy and tears fall like rain.
Once in a lifetime, will you find such a blessing,
Now you are not here, it is so distressing.
And it is, I don't know what to do next,
I behave like a moron and speak out of text,
And I stammer, I have lost all my glamour,
Each time my heart beats, it feels like a hammer,
In my chest, I thought you knew best,
Now you are angry and I am depressed.
What's the matter? What has gone wrong,
Please hurry back to where you belong.

Madeline Morris

A Haiku Promise - Lo, I Am With You Always

At the touch of frost
Soft blooming petals curl and die;
Not so my love.

As life's passion cools
And times grow hard and hair turns grey,
Stays firm my love.

Then, at the ending,
Though fear enthrall'd, submerge that fear
In this my love.

Abide then ever,
Where e'er thou far'st, in life or death,
Safe in my love.

G A Baker

REPEATED REPETITION

*Love and beauty: a sonnet song for
the entrancing Ann-maryllis*

Why oh why, I wonder, why do I?
At some unbidden moment every day,
In bed perhaps, at work, or on the motorway
Repeatedly repeat the words that fly
Through my enraptured mind, called into play
By some swift unrelated thought, indeed
At times with little thought at all. Quite freed
Of all deliberate intent, they simply say
Precisely what they mean: no apt device
Of literature hangs in to give them force
And they themselves, one potent source
I stand by poetry's endless quest for paradise.
What say they then, these words so brief, so true?
They say: Dear Ann-maryllis, I love you.

Perhaps it's how you sometimes turn your head,
Or maybe a swift movement as you take
Your seat; a gesture even you might make
In conversation, captured by a thread
Of light, how can I tell? Yet in a flash
As swift and bright as lightning my eyes
Are dazzled by a glimpse of beauty that defies
My power to describe; it makes me catch
My breath, for this is loveliness that lies
Engraved deep in my core, mine, unique,
A vision that a perfect match must seek
Before it shows its face and in my eyes
Could never be eclipsed in beauty seen
By others, were it that of Sheba's Queen.

Frank Littlewood

DISTANCES

Distances can be measured,
In feet, fathoms, and miles.
But also by heartache.

How many miles to Timbuktu?
How deep is the ocean?
How high is the sky?
How long is a bungee jump?
How far to the moon?

Now you have distanced yourself
To a place a long, long way from me,
Where I cannot go.
I am bereft.
I cannot touch your body,
Kiss your lips, or stroke your hair.
Rejection is very hard to bear,
When it comes from someone you love.

Eve M Turner

I Could Only Stand And Stare

The sun shone down from Heaven
Upon your golden hair,
A mighty ray of light it wove,
And I could only stand and stare.

The moon shone down from Heaven
As you were lying there.
It spread its beams upon the Earth,
And I could only stand and stare.

The stars shone down from Heaven
Upon your cheek so fair.
I knew that you had breathed your last,
And I could only stand and stare.

Then darkness came upon the Earth,
And hid your face so rare.
I saw your body laid to rest -
And I could only stand and stare.

Mary Baird Hammond

ECHOES

Echoes,
Without a menace,
Just a cool relaxed vibe
On a summer's evening
As the sounds rise from the street.

I'm looking down from an open window
Almost as an unnoticed observer
My eyes and ears dart from
Movement to movement
Sound to sound

There's crockery
There's cutlery
Being moved
And the clinking of glasses
Being raised as a toast
To times and friends like these

Voices
Rise from a suspicious murmur
To an unbridled tide of mirth
Someone's cracking jokes
Fuelled by some wine or spirit.

There are couples
Making it clear
Just where their intentions lie
They'll slip away
While others still angle to make their play
To try and cross the finishing line

As the night slips away
The die-hards are still raising glasses
Still regaling tales of yore
These echoes will die away
And I'll be left with these memories.

Richard Gould

TOO LITTLE TOO LATE

My beautiful baby boy
So precious and so new
But God looked down and took you back.
He said Planet Earth is not for you.
God must have had his reasons,
And I know they would be true.
But to this day sweetheart
I still grieve for you.
You have never been forgotten
You are always in my mind,
I sing a little song for you
Tears well up in my eyes.
I held you for just one moment
Then you were gone for good,
I never said goodbye to you
The way I know I should,
I never brought a flower
I do not even know why you went
You were a darling little bud
To me from heaven-sent,
If I had been a grown-up
I would have understood
And done things very differently,
Done everything I could,
But I was just a child in grief,
I did not want to look
I could not bear to see,
There's nothing I can ever do,
To put things right I know.
So I keep this pain inside for you
I don't want to let it go.

Jill Lowe

I'VE LOVED A FEW TIMES

I've loved a few times
Must have found the wrong ones
Love was sweet at first
But then became thorns in my side
I thought he was the one
He treated me bad, and it made me sad
Once I felt like an everlasting flower
That would never close up
With nectar that was sweet
Then it withered away
Someone I loved, I thought would stay
Love's not a game to play
People die of broken hearts along the way
So love can be a bunch of roses
Or nasty thorns in your side
So if you're the one,
That's lucky in love
Your love will feel forever
Like buds of flowers,
Forever opening up.

M Woolvin

BEAUTY - I'VE SEEN THE RAREST BEAUTY OF ALL

She is such a beautiful woman
So graceful a lady is she
Each movement is so true
Oh Lord, please make me half my age.

Without my aches and pains
And I would fight any duel to win her hand
And crush any barriers in my way
For her beauty is not just skin deep.

As in her face you see the real beauty
The gentleness that's hard to believe
The softness that is hard to explain
And the dream that's in her eyes.

This is the real beauty that's within
For I have only seen this beauty once before
Oh this beautiful lady has stole my heart
For this beautiful lady has the sweetest smile I've seen.

Now what should I to do, what dare I do?
Ask this lovely lady for her hand in marriage
Love really does hurt, knowing if I did
That I could only hurt this lady because of my age, love hurts.

Keith Jackson

DIE FOR LOVE

Among the sheets
The stirred boy sleeps;
Dreaming dreams
. . . At once, he screams.

Languished by love,
The anguish, he' sick of;
For the end he reaches
And his heart, it screeches.

The poison he drinks,
His body, it shrinks.
Upon his bed, the healed boy lies
And out the window, his seraphic soul flies.

Natalie Biagioni (15)

BLIND DATE

Piccadilly Station platform forty-two
I looked around in the bar,
Glancing in every direction -
Please don't let it be him - or him - or him
I'm dressed as I said, which one is you
My eyes widely open, glistening with fear.
No description fit, I'm out of here.
Bustling and fumbling for my ticket and a quick exit home.
Banged arm in arm into a man.
Prematurely grey and six feet tall.
Sorry in unison as I rubbed my elbow
He rubbed it too, I flinched
Sorry he said for touching
Are you alright?
Six years on now, my best friend
And the love of my life.

A Hyde Murphy

TAKE NOTE

Take notice of your dreams
Vivid, glorious to the wild extremes
Don't worry about your man's need
To digress, to impress
Go brave, go forward, get more
Than your bra off your sensual breast
More than combined limbs
Dancing together towards sleep
Shadows in firelight
Candlelight keep
The secret of passion
The gentle gesture
Secret the joy of being together
Sill and calm on the surface
A furnace beneath
If it's a secret why care what others believe
We do
We know
It is our truth
It has to be enough
The best we can do, is love.

Sue Woodbine

SHE PINES

If I look at you too long
I shall never look away.
But I fear that I am wrong
And it isn't mine to say.

There is wonder in your spirit
Loved you first time I saw.
Want so much to say it
But this fear just clamps my jaw.

I could watch you every hour
And simply drink you in.
Knocked sideways by this power
And I wonder, is it sin?

Can't say what you have inside
That has taken me apart.
There is no place that I can hide
You have landed in my heart.

I dream of being close to you
To hold you all night through.
There is no guide on what to do
Than how I feel being true.

J E Kirkman

SORROW HOLLOW

There is a hollow called Sorrow,
Where it rains until tomorrow,
Stop your broken heart I'll borrow,
It's a tale of love, won and lost,
Broken promises and teardrops are its cost,
It's a land of unrequited love,
And if your hand fits this glove,
Pause this way and weep,
Two naked couples fast asleep,
Love's garments case aside in a heap,
A broken vow you cannot keep,
After all still waters run deep,
And above all you cannot swim,
So why are you still in love with him?

Alan Pow

FRAGILE

How beautiful and wondrous
The snowflake must have felt;
Prismatic are its filigrees;
How quickly it does melt.

How delicate the cut glass;
Its patterns so well spoken;
Thin flowers etched about it;
How easily it is broken.

A tender love is like that,
When built of wishes, frail;
Can blossom in an instant,
And in an instant fail.

With secrets kept in silence,
And emotions kept inside,
I raised the knife of cruel words;
With fatal wounds, love died.

John Bilven Morin

EMPTY THE DAY

Empty the day with you not there
Wittering on at my side,
Telling me off for things that I said
Helping me out when I cried.

Believing in me when all I could see
Were hopeless scenarios,
And all the still while keeping your smile
To hide what nobody knows.

Hard battles with life resulted in strife
But we have many joys too,
For our little ones and their children did
Help us to make it through.

A beauty I found in winning you round
I don't think you had the best deal,
It seems such a waste with all your good taste
But thankfully I had a steal.

I wish I could be as much to you
As you have been sure to me,
And hope the good Lord could take it on board
To not take us separately.

Nigel Davies

HEARTBREAK'S LIGHT

The sun sets on another day,
Your heart begins to fade, to weep;
Once more love slips into the night.
Your grief is lasting and so deep
At regrets, a taste so bitter.
Your pain unending, your life grey,
The future suddenly takes flight.

The sun has set upon your love,
But merely await within sleep
For sunsets all bring sunrises.

See, a new dawn creeps into sight.

Marty Grief

SPACE

You and your things have lived with me here,
In gentle harmony for year upon year.
Scuffed shoes and sandals for your quiet brown feet,
Jeans and soft shirts to cover your body, muscled but neat.
A hat and a scarf, some gloves for your masculine hands.
A heaped pile of change, keys, sweets, pale elastic bands.
CDs, newspapers, magazines, photos the essence of you
I foolishly thought these things meant your love would stay true.
Now you and your things live in someone else's place
And I am left here with acres of space.
Space all around that tortures and taunts
Space in my thoughts your warm memory haunts.
A desert of space that tortures but can't kill
And space in my heart that no one can fill.

Carol Spencer

A Summer Rhapsody

O beauty mine, give me my just reward;
Restore to me the nectar of your love,
And send the old transgressions passionward,
Transfigured in the likeness of a dove.

Your naked innocence was my desire,
Your adolescent bloom was my repose,
And your heart was consumed in my heart's fire,
As love consumes the crimson in the rose.

And you languished at the heart of things,
Concealed in rapture, like a hidden prayer;
You bade me welcome, and with love's soft wings,
I entered on your shining presence there.

Since then, the flood of years has borne away
The ecstasies that sealed your lips with mine,
And now I muse along the golden way
Of memory, devoid of lovers' wine.

Thus must I wander till at last I die,
And I shall go, pursued by one regret:
That I fell short of you, and don't know why -
Perhaps you haunt the old misgivings yet.

S H Smith

END OF THE GAME

You say that you really love me,
And it would be such a great shame.
If you were too blind to notice,
I'm starting to tire of the game.

You made too many promises,
And your excuses were so lame.
You didn't keep any of them,
I'm starting to tire of the game.

When we first met I was on fire,
You were the one to light my flame.
But now you blow hot and then cold,
I'm starting to tire of the game.

Now I see how selfish you are,
I waited but you never came.
You think I will always forgive,
I'm starting to tire of the game.

You have such a massive ego,
And believe I swoon at your name.
But baby I've got news for you,
I'm starting to tire of the game.

You played with my emotions,
But my spirit you'll never tame.
I'm not the fool you thought I was,
I'm starting to tire of the game.

You've blown it and now it's over,
You've only got yourself to blame.
I gave you so many chances,
But now it's the end of the game.

Ann Blair

THE LOWEST TIME OF MY LIFE

I can write how I feel each time you've broken my heart
But if I had to speak my thoughts I don't know where to start
I can remember on many occasions the times that you've declined
To share your love for me: what goes on inside your mind?

I wonder if the tables were turned, would you put up with this?
Months of blaming yourself for the loving that's been missed
To feel some warmth in your soul, I've looked but I cannot see
How to light the spark we had when you fell in love with me.

I felt complete the day you asked me to be your wife
But there's a part of us that's missing to complete this happy life
I think of others being loved the way you once loved me
If I were brave, I'd speak these thoughts: give you the chance to
                                                    make me happy.

Louise Allen

RECITAL

Listening,
I heard
A beautiful song,
Sweet as a rose,
Melodic
Over and over.
My eyes closed,
Words
They danced along,
By the crafted hand.
Imagination
Askilled its purpose.
Each line
Wept,
Each verse
An eye
Touched.

Christopher W Wolfe

How Can I?

How can I continue going on
Without you in my life?
How can I continue being strong
Without you by my side?
What if we left to somewhere new,
A quiet life just me and you?
I want to have you to myself.
I want to feel only you and no one else.

How can I continue this way,
As you lead me more and more astray?
How can I have done something so wrong?
How can it feel so right?
Why don't we run away, and chase our dreams
To suit our needs?
I want to be with you, I want us to grow.
I want to be free with you and lose control.

Danielle Watts

I'M UNDER YOUR SPELL

I thought you would let me go
our fire still burns bright
I thought this wasn't so
you've made me full of delight
You know darling
you have made me feel that I'm alive
I live for you, you see
without you my world would die
I thought you would miss me
loving you has made me strong
You see I'm under your spell
deep down you can tell
How much our love means
doesn't matter how far it seems
we are in each other's thoughts
Nothing can make us feel distraught
we have got each other once more
I know you will come
knocking again on my door
I love to love you
I enjoy your pleasure
Alone, I feel for you
holding on to my treasure.

Patricia Green

ELEGY TO LOVE

No amount of wondering can make rehearse
    For that exalted moment when
Something brightens in her eyes, and senses nurse
    The chance to fall in love again.
Love was like the aftermath of some trench war
    Where all the preparations were
Impotent against a mighty foe that tore
    The ranks apart and left just her.

Love was like the aftermath of some trench war
    Bewildering those gentle scenes
Formed from fine romantic images before
    I learnt what real emotion means.
Like forgotten men whose identities drift
    Away with any sense of mind,
When the bugle blew so life from death could sift
    All lay unknowing, sick and blind.

Like forgotten men whose identities drift
    Who knows if love was won or lost?
All I had was some vague sense of some great gift
    And medals with my name embossed.
Small wonder then that men fear to love, so hide
    The depth of what they can achieve.
If only women knew how we felt inside
    They may love more and grant reprieve.

Fraser Hicks

ETERNAL DESIRE

You are my eternal desire
And I need you.
You set my heart on fire
And I love you.

But what can I do?
I need you tonight.
Drink is such a bore
And TV is no delight.

But what can I do
To ease my fright?
I feel so sad because
You're not here tonight.

I need your love again
And I know you need me.
My heart's in so much pain
And I wish you'd want me.

Peter Steele

WITHOUT YOU

Without you,
There would be no me,
Without you,
There would be no poetry,
Without your love,
There would be no reality.

Without pain,
There would be no gain,
Without war,
There would be no peace
And without revenge,
There would be no release.

Without sin,
There would be no good,
Without trust,
There would be no blood.
Without life,
There would be no strife,
Without your heart,
There would be no start.

Without your smile,
There would be no sun,
Without you here,
There would be no fun.

Without your eyes,
There would be no light,
Without your voice,
There would be no night.

Yes, without you,
There would be no me,
Without your love,
There would be no poetry
And without you,
There would be no reality.

Julia Smith

WHEN TWO BECOME ONE

Come to me Robert my love
Please use mine eyes and ears
Reach down deep within your heart
And spread love where once was tears

Our spirits will become entwined
When two at last become one
Our Father's hand will then bless us both
All heartache then will be gone

The world will be as spirits joined
His children full of glee
At last the world will reunite
With Father's love so free.

April Dickinson-Owen

A Love Affair

How could I not you love?
With such a face I did you take
Into my life, like a pure dove.
Dropping a feather like a snowflake.
When we were in love together,
I always had this strange feeling.
As if you could even change the weather,
Because snow became sun in our dealing.
Then we had to be so far apart,
As you went off to that war to fight.
Pine I did, that you wouldn't forsake my heart,
For in your danger, there was never any delight.
Returning, did you know how much you were missed?
Until I fell into your arms, in love again, being kissed.

Marjorie Busby

HEARTSEASE

The heart was not formed to be broken;
Words spoken denying
This provoking thought,
Flash and are lost
In a hoaxing, self indulgent
Refulgent lie.

Our emotions, spectrally analysed,
Show colours from cortex medulla,
Hormone flux, and maybe
Sheer gut costive melancholy.

Meanwhile, the sun went down
In crimson opalescent glory,
Unmatched except in distant memory.

Geraint Jenkins

TEMPTATION OF AN ORANGE

An orange beckoned from the dish
With anticipation he licked his lips
First dispense with outer covering
To reach the succulent flesh within
With all her top later now removed
She lay there in creamy underclothes
He was so gentle with the pith
He didn't realise he drooled a bit
Then he reached her gossamer skin
Holding her firm, fleshy fruit within
Next he relished the tangy taste
Explode in his mouth, not a drop did he waste
All too soon the orange was gone
And he was left with a skin all torn.

Juliet Marshall

AUTOBIOGRAPHY

For most of my life I've favoured it,
The drooling showed I'd savoured it.
I don't think I abused it,
I never once refused it.
I've always loved the stuff of it,
And never got enough of it.
I don't think it's illegal,
To procure it by inveigle.
It's thrilling when it's proffered,
Delightful when it's offered
When bodies touch and so enmesh,
To sense the closeness of the flesh,
It's then we feel that we are burning
The waiting then was worth the yearning.
The sense of joy will culminate,
When each will satisfy their mate.
Although it may be in my blood,
I'll not become a common stud.
In prowess, with enough to show
A penchant for a gigolo
My attitude at times was flirty,
Though never deemed coitus dirty

Look at the time it's half-past two,
I think it's time we had a brew.

But then again, we're still on heat,
I'm sure you'd welcome a repeat.
Wow!

Bill Austin

THE MAGNET

Through the glaring footlights and the smoky haze
A thousand female eyes, upon my body gaze
Here I stand alone, the centre of attraction
With a feeling of well being and a smile of satisfaction
My muscles hard and strong, ripple on every limb
From endless hours of workouts, at the local gym
Giving me the confidence to do what I do best
As kindly Mother Nature, gave me all the rest
The adrenaline starts to flow, my whole body through
My routine music plays, (to be sung) *Let me entertain you.*

Women stand on tables, screaming out things wild
It seems so long ago now, they were thought as meek and mild
The atmosphere has changed them, from waiting impatiently
Into a frenzied horde, they even paid a fee
I hold them totally spellbound, I feel their body heat
Yet never a second glance, would I get in the street
Why my body is a magnet it's difficult to explain
As I move in ever closer, I drive them all insane
Their perfumes fill my nostrils, their hands begin to move
Across my glistening body, slender fingers slowly rove.

Reluctantly I pull away so everyone can see
The reason why I'm here, that vital part of me
I turn my back to tease them, my thong falls to the floor
They urge me on to turn; to show them even more
Clapping their hands to the music, I also keep in time
Swinging my dangling phallus in any sort of line
I leap down from the stage, their hands reach out to touch
Anything they can, mine protect my crutch
Running back to my changing room for fear I'll lose my life
Dress back again as a nobody, and return to my sweet wife.

Clive Goldsmith

ANIMAL INSTINCT

Butterflies caress my back as you walk in.
Dolphins dive in my stomach.
Bears snuggle me as you come closer.
You touch me and all the animals in the zoo escape and go wild!
Mine's the tiger.

Theresa Griffiths

SUZANNE

I do not want your soul -
that endless part of you.
A tasteless spring; no warmth,
or sound,
no laughter bending truth.

I do not want your soul -
that absence in your eyes,
where concentration, comfort lived,
and life was lighting fires.

I do not love your soul,
and crave your smile despite,
and fingers in my hair,
and bruises on your thighs.

I do not want your soul
where secrets and lies begin.
I love your body bare,
and breath breaking breath
on buttered skin.

I do not want your soul,
but a happiness that inherits homes
with sugar bowls and glasses filled,
being noticed when alone.

I do not want your soul -
can't hear its troubled truth,
no matter how it screams or sings;
I do not want your soul my love, it's more,
my soul wants you.

Kevin Hayhoe

INFORMATION

We hope you have enjoyed reading this book - and that you will continue to enjoy it in the coming years.

If you like reading and writing poetry drop us a line, or give us a call, and we'll send you a free information pack.

Alternatively if you would like to order further copies of this book or any of our other titles, then please give us a call or log onto our website at www.forwardpress.co.uk

**Anchor Books Information
Remus House
Coltsfoot Drive
Peterborough
PE2 9JX
(01733) 898102**